Thanks San Francisco Digital for the animations.

Special thanks to my wife, Teresa Wrenn, and
Danielle Wrenn for assisting with the
revision of the manuscript.

CORPY

THE LITTLE RED
CORPUSCLE

"HI! I'M CORPY, I AM A
RED BLOOD CELL."

"THERE ARE 2.5 TRILLION
RED BLOOD CELLS JUST LIKE
ME IN THE HUMAN BODY."

"I WAS BORN HERE, IN THE
FEMUR. THE FEMUR IS A
BONE IN YOUR LEG. "

"TODAY IS A BIG DAY. IT'S MY
FIRST DAY GOING TO WORK
IN THE HUMAN BODY!"

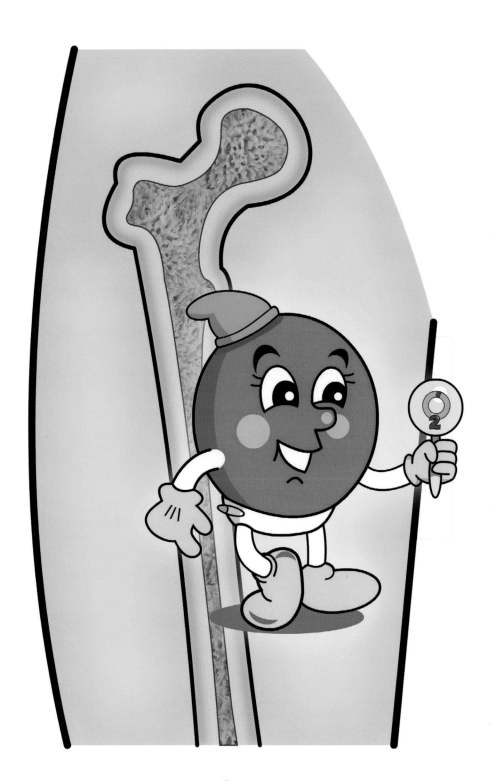

"MY FIRST STOP IS THE HEART.
BUT HOW DO I GET THERE?
I'LL LOOK AT MY MAP."

"OH! THAT'S RIGHT! I'LL TRAVEL
THROUGH THE VENA CAVA."

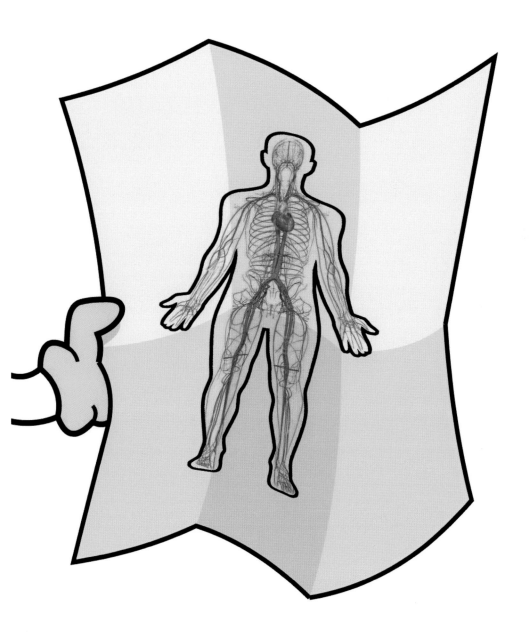

"THE INFERIOR VENA CAVA IS
A LARGE VEIN WHICH CARRIES
BLOOD FROM THE LOWER
BODY BACK TO THE HEART."

"THE SUPERIOR VENA CAVA IS
A LARGE VEIN WHICH CARRIES
BLOOD FROM THE UPPER
BODY BACK TO THE HEART."

VEINS AND ARTERIES ARE LIKE
HIGHWAYS THAT TAKE BLOOD
CELLS ALL OVER THE HUMAN BODY.

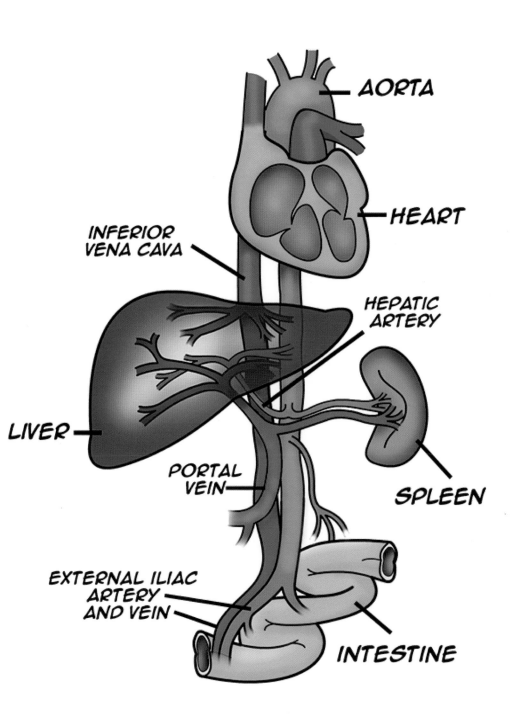

AORTA

HEART

INFERIOR
VENA CAVA

HEPATIC
ARTERY

LIVER

PORTAL
VEIN

SPLEEN

EXTERNAL ILIAC
ARTERY
AND VEIN

INTESTINE

"I MADE IT TO
THE HEART!"

"THE HEART IS LIKE
A TRAIN STATION."

"A RED BLOOD CELL,
LIKE ME, CAN GO
ANYWHERE IN THE
HUMAN BODY FROM
THE HEART."

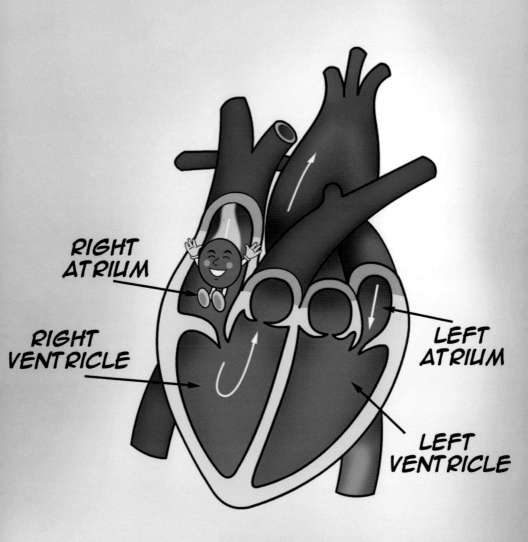

"NOW I NEED TO GET SOME OXYGEN."

"TO OBTAIN OXYGEN I MUST TRAVEL
FROM THE HEART TO THE LUNGS."

"OXYGEN COMES FROM THE AIR THAT
WE BREATHE AND IS AVAILABLE IN
THE LUNGS. ONE OF MY JOBS IS TO
CARRY OXYGEN FROM THE LUNGS
TO ALL PARTS OF THE BODY."

"MY OTHER JOB IS TO REMOVE
CARBON DIOXIDE FROM ALL PARTS OF
THE BODY AND TO TAKE THE CARBON
DIOXIDE BACK TO THE LUNGS."

"AFTER PICKING UP OXYGEN
FROM THE LUNGS, I MUST RETURN
TO THE HEART TO BE PUMPED
WITH OTHER BLOOD CELLS TO
ALL PARTS OF THE BODY."

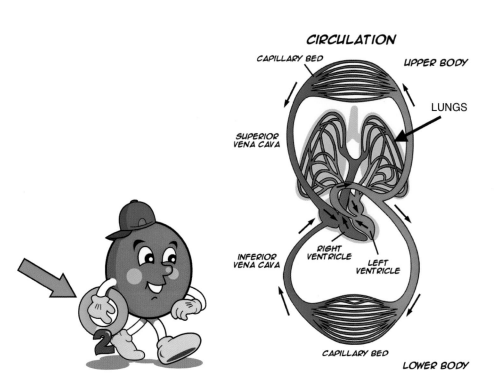

"FROM THE LUNGS I TRAVEL FIRST TO THE LEFT ATRIUM AND THEN TO THE LEFT VENTRICLE."

"FROM THE LEFT VENTRICLE I AM PUMPED WITH OTHER CELLS INTO THE AORTA ."

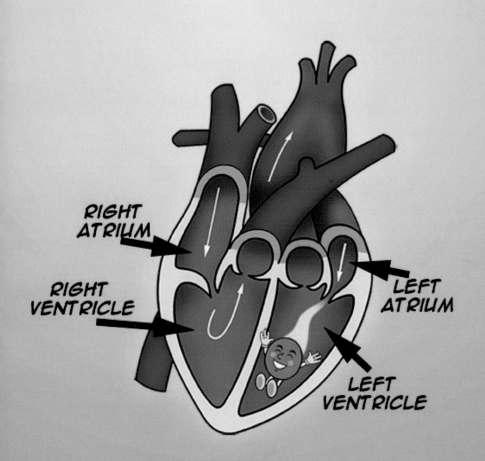

"FROM THE AORTA I CAN TRAVEL WITH OTHER
BLOOD CELLS TO ALL PARTS OF THE BODY."

"HMMM. I WONDER WHERE I
SHOULD TAKE THIS OXYGEN."

"HI THERE, I'M LUCY! I'M A
WHITE BLOOD CELL."

"HI, I'M CORPY, I AM A NEW RED BLOOD
CELL. THIS IS MY FIRST DAY ON THE JOB.
WHAT DOES A WHITE BLOOD CELL DO?"

"WHITE BLOOD CELLS ARE PART OF
THE IMMUNE SYSTEM. WE HELP THE
HUMAN BODY TO FIGHT INFECTION
FROM BACTERIA AND VIRUSES."

"WOW! SOUNDS LIKE IMPORTANT WORK!

MAYBE YOU CAN HELP ME. I WAS WONDERING
WHERE TO TAKE THIS OXYGEN."

"WHY DON'T YOU TAKE THE O_2 TO THE BRAIN?
FOLLOW THE AORTA TO THE INTERNAL CAROTID
ARTERIES WHICH LEAD TO THE BRAIN."

"I SHALL, THANKS!"

"BUT FIRST, LET ME TELL YOU
ABOUT THE BRAIN..."

"THE HUMAN BRAIN IS DIVIDED INTO THREE PARTS:"

1. THE NEW BRAIN OR THE CEREBRUM

2. THE MIDBRAIN

3. THE OLD BRAIN OR THE LIMBIC SYSTEM"

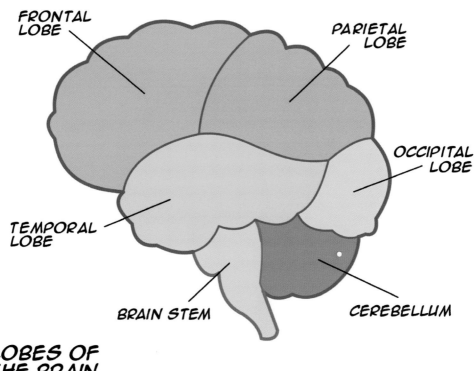

FRONTAL LOBE

PARIETAL LOBE

OCCIPITAL LOBE

TEMPORAL LOBE

BRAIN STEM

CEREBELLUM

LOBES OF THE BRAIN

Image page 18

"WOW! THE BRAIN IS A PRETTY COOL PLACE. THIS IS THE CONTROL CENTER OF THE ENTIRE HUMAN BODY. LOBES ARE THE DIFFERENT PARTS OF THE BRAIN AND THEY WORK TOGETHER TO TELL THE BODY WHAT TO DO."

"TO WHICH PART OF THE BRAIN SHOULD I TAKE THIS OXYGEN?"

"HELLO THERE! I COULD USE SOME OXYGEN OVER HERE IN THE OLD BRAIN."

"HERE'S SOME OXYGEN FOR YOU. BEFORE I GO, WILL YOU TELL ME WHAT THE OLD BRAIN DOES?"

"THE OLD BRAIN CONTROLS ALL OF THE BODY'S BASIC FUNCTIONS; LIKE BREATHING, SLEEPING, AND EATING."

"THE OLD BRAIN ALLOWS A PERSON TO QUICKLY DECIDE ON LIKES AND DISLIKES."

"WHAT DO YOU DISLIKE?"

"I DO NOT LIKE CIGARETTE SMOKING, AIR POLLUTION, LOUD MUSIC...!

"EXCUSE ME, I MUST LEAVE NOW."

"OH! BEFORE YOU LEAVE, I HAVE SOME CARBON DIOXIDE THAT YOU CAN TAKE FOR ME."

"THE OLD BRAIN GAVE ME SOME CARBON DIOXIDE TO TAKE BACK TO THE LUNGS."

"CARBON DIOXIDE (CO_2) IS WHAT'S LEFT OVER AFTER THE BODY USES OXYGEN."

"WHEW! THIS HAS BEEN A LONG DAY OF WORK."

"THANKS FOR COMING WITH ME ON MY FIRST DAY OF WORK!"

"COME WITH ME ON MY NEXT ADVENTURE AND MEET ALL MY FRIENDS WHO LIVE AND CIRCULATE THROUGH THE HUMAN BODY."